Original title:
Feathers for the Soul

Copyright © 2025 Creative Arts Management OÜ
All rights reserved.

Author: Eleanor Prescott
ISBN HARDBACK: 978-1-80586-117-1
ISBN PAPERBACK: 978-1-80586-589-6

Soft Shadows of Tomorrow

In dreams we jump like silly frogs,
With marshmallows stuck on our sogs.
We chase the clouds and tickle the sky,
With plans so grand, they might just fly.

A potato flew around my room,
It danced to tunes of techno boom.
With every twirl, it made me laugh,
I thought of a duck in a bubble bath.

Tomorrow's mischiefs hide in the breeze,
Whispering secrets, like sneaky bees.
On cotton candy clouds we prance,
Wearing hats of cereal, we take a chance.

So bring your socks and your silly grin,
Let's spin and sway, let the fun begin!
With goofy giggles, we'll sail away,
In a sea of silliness, come what may.

Chasing Sunlight on Silken Wings

We waltz on rainbows, in flip-flops bright,
Chasing the sunlight, oh what a sight!
With ice cream hats and silly tunes,
We dance around like a bunch of loons.

A squirrel in sunglasses steals the show,
Painting the air with a colorful glow.
While owls hoot, sharing jokes at night,
A giggle brigade, taking flight!

We swing from branches, in pure delight,
Hopping like kangaroos, taking flight.
On silken wings, we soar so high,
With laughter echoing, we touch the sky.

So join this party, let's make some fun,
With a dash of silliness, we always run.
In sunlight's arms, we'll forever chase,
With smiles so bright, we'll fill the space.

Inked in Airy Echoes

Giggly whispers dance in flight,
Inky thoughts take off at night.
A banter written in the breeze,
Humor sprinkles through the trees.

Clouds parade in silly array,
Jokes are stitched in bright display.
Laughter floats on wings so high,
A canvas where the giggles sigh.

The Spirit's Feathered Glow

A sparkly giggle, a feathered grin,
Laughter spills where dreams begin.
Whimsical fancies gently tease,
A ticklish heart floats with ease.

Gooey joy in bubbly tones,
The spirit jives with silly drones.
Echoes pitter-pat around,
In a giggle forest, we're spellbound.

Feathers of Hope Cradled in Light

A cozy warmth with every quirk,
Hope's plush wings give dreams a smirk.
Tickling thoughts, they rustle near,
A feathered chuckle, oh so clear.

Witty whispers drift on by,
Bouncing dreams kiss the sky.
Happiness entwined in flight,
Silly giggles in the light.

Skyward Dreams and Gentle Shadows

Upward flights of silly schemes,
Dancing on our joy-filled dreams.
Shadows giggle, tickling the sun,
Whippity laughs, a hop and run.

Swaying, laughing, the clouds conspire,
Whims and fancies never tire.
Floating high, we play all day,
In laugh-filled skies, we'll always stay.

Surrender to the Drift

Balloons danced in the breeze,
Like squirrels in a tutu,
A ladybug took a dive,
To join a picnic review.

We tossed our doubts to the wind,
And rolled on grassy falls,
Laughter echoed through the trees,
As joy kicked down the walls.

Hues of Transcendence

A banana peel on my shoe,
Is the color of my grace,
As I tumble through the park,
With a smile on my face.

The sky's painted with a wink,
As clouds all giggle a tune,
Jumping jacks in twilight hue,
Making scenes beneath the moon.

The Unseen Touch of Kindness

A cat purred like a motor,
As I danced in my slippers,
It plotted a scheme of antics,
While I stumbled on my quippers.

A warm hug from a breeze,
Made my afternoon sprout,
Like a dandelion laughing,
As the sun shouts, 'Go out!'

A Symphony in the Sky

Pigeons rocked their heads to beats,
In a concert of silly birds,
With a harp made of windchimes,
And chorus sung without words.

The moon tapped a jazzy foot,
As stars wished they could sing,
While meteors stole the show,
In a dazzling cosmic fling.

The Weight of Airy Fantasies

In dreams I fly with a taco hat,
Sipping clouds made of bubble gum.
My worries drift like a cheerful cat,
Time to dance on dreams and have some fun.

Balloons carry my socks on high,
They giggle and wiggle, oh what a sight!
With each puff of breeze, I touch the sky,
Chasing chubby clouds, what a delight!

Plumes of Hope on the Horizon

Jelly beans float on rainbow waves,
While unicorns sip soda, what a tease!
A circus of pancakes, oh how it behaves,
A world where everything is a breeze.

I ride on the back of a playful kite,
Tickling the stars with popcorn and cheer.
In giggly whispers, the moon shines bright,
Happiness wrapped in a giant sphere!

Threads of the Ethereal

My spaghetti dreams twirl and spin,
With meatballs dancing on fluffy clouds.
I wear a jacket made of penguin skin,
Making snow angels that laugh out loud.

Lollipops jive with a jellybean crew,
While marshmallow clouds throw a cake parade.
In this wacky world, nothing's taboo,
Where every silliness is lovingly laid.

The Gentle Sweep of the Wind

A butterfly wearing tiny shoes,
Dances in spaces where giggles roam.
With whispers of joy, it sings the blues,
Tickling the flowers, calling them home.

The breeze tosses hats with a playful wink,
As squirrels juggle apples with squeaky glee.
In this dance of joy, there's no time to think,
Just laughter and fun, forever carefree!

The Dance of Ethereal Down

In a world of fluff and giggles,
The clouds wear socks, what funny wiggles!
A chicken moon takes center stage,
While laughter spills like ink from page.

Birds in bow ties, how they strut,
Chasing dreams, while hopping in a rut!
With every flap, they change the beat,
A jig of joy, can't feel defeat.

The breeze plays tricks, it's hard to hold,
As pranks unfold, both brave and bold.
With every twirl, a chuckle bursts,
In the air, it's laughter that thrusts.

So come and join this airy spree,
Where shadows dance, and spirits are free.
No need for rules, just float along,
In this whimsical world, we all belong!

Threads of Light in Twilight

In the dusk, the giggles thread,
With sparkles dancing, pink and red.
Silly shadows chase the light,
As stars wear hats, a comical sight.

A bubble burst, the laugh escapes,
Ticklish whispers, spun from shapes.
With grace, the twilight jests and bows,
And twirls 'round trees with comical vows.

Glimmers land on noses bright,
As owls do jokes, just to ignite.
The moon slips on its brightest socks,
While nighttime laughs like some old fox.

So let us dive in hues of cheer,
With threads of light that bring us near.
In every giggle, we find a spark,
In this twilight, let's leave our mark!

Ascent of the Spirit's Wing

Up we fly like cream on cocoa,
With a whoosh and giggle—what a show!
The skies ignite with playful shouts,
As spirits soar, there are no doubts.

Balloons are jokes, upon the breeze,
Laughing loud in the trees with ease.
With every flap, joy fills the air,
As we twirl about without a care.

Clouds tiptoe past, like old-time peers,
While starlight tickles, dissolving fears.
Up in the heights, how silly we look,
Floating through life, let's write the book!

So laugh with the wind, and fly so high,
In every giggle, we paint the sky.
With each ascent, let's chase delight,
In this dance of wonder, all feels right!

A Symphony in Shades of Air

In swirling hues, the laughter plays,
A symphony beckons in joyful ways.
With trumpets made of bubbles and cheer,
Each note a giggle, crystal clear.

The wind strums softly on tree stringed sails,
As clouds twirl about with feathered tales.
Every rustle a rhythm, every breeze a rhyme,
Creating soundscapes, dancing through time.

Around us play a cast of light,
Singing songs of whimsy through the night.
Where dreams jive and silliness reigns,
In this symphony, we break all chains.

Come join the tune, let's float and sway,
In shades of air, we'll laugh and play.
In this dance of joy, let spirits align,
Where every chuckle is truly divine!

Canvas of Lightness

In a world of goofy flight,
Birds wear hats, oh what a sight!
With painted wings, they take to air,
Leaving giggles everywhere.

A canvas stretched with silly schemes,
Colorful clouds in playful beams.
Pigeons prance, don't take a stance,
Dancing birds in a silly dance.

Fish in bow ties swim along,
Joining in this feathered song.
What a ruckus, what a fuss,
Nature's humor, a vibrant plus!

A laugh shared, a wink and twirl,
In the sky, let laughter swirl.
A canvas full of joy and jest,
Where lightness roams, we feel the best.

A Skyward Embrace

Up in the air where goofballs glide,
Nuts in chapeaus, quite the ride!
Squirrels giggle with wings spread wide,
In fluffy clouds, they softly bide.

Sketching smiles in endless blue,
With chocolate chip clouds, not one or two.
Birds dressed silly, flying so high,
Kissing the sun, waving goodbye.

Launching giggles where giggles belong,
A topsy-turvy, plucky dance throng.
With laughter lifting spirits anew,
We twirl through skies, who knew we could do?

Embrace the lightness, let humor soar,
Don't be surprised if birds ask for more.
In every flutter, in each tight hug,
The humor sparkles, as we air-snug.

Echoes of the Lighter Heart

Whimsical whispers in the breeze,
Feathered friends dance with such ease.
Chirpy jokes on a sunlit spree,
A heart so light, full of glee.

Dive into laughter, never apart,
In every chuckle, the world is smart.
Wings flapping, laughter framing the sky,
Joking clouds drift and thumb their eye.

Tickled pink, the world goes round,
Silly echoes of joy abound.
A festival of quirks in every beat,
Filling up life with rhymes so sweet.

Swinging on air like it's a ride,
Every flutter is a joyful slide.
Echoes bouncing in rainbow hues,
Crafting fun stories in vibrant views.

Gossamer Dreams in Flight

Twinkling stars in a food parade,
Puff pastry clouds in a grand charade.
With gossamer wings, all spirits gleam,
Floating along in a whimsical dream.

Bumblebees buzzing in tiny hats,
Telling tales like chitchatting cats.
With cotton candy trails to trot,
Every adventure's a giggle spot.

Inventive creatures float around,
Mixing giggles with a bouncy sound.
Each little wink, a gift to keep,
In the light of laughter, the soul leaps.

Gossamer visions, brightly bright,
In every moment, pure delight.
Dreams taking flight, a joyous chase,
In the dance of joy, we find our place.

Gliding Through Infinite Dreams

In dreams, I ride a fluffy cloud,
With giggles loud, I feel so proud.
A flock of ducks in ballet gear,
Twirl around, let's give a cheer!

The stars play hide-and-seek at night,
While I sip lemonade, oh what a sight!
A comet's tail tickles my nose,
As laughter in the cosmos grows.

Balloons float by with wings so bright,
They serenade me with delight.
I chase them down, oh what a race,
Dancing through the galactic space!

In this world so absurdly grand,
I bounce on marshmallows, oh so planned.
With dreams like this, I'm free to roam,
Silly giggles lead me home.

Women of the Wild Wind

Oh, women bold with hats so grand,
They tip their feathers on the sand.
Riding gusts like wild mustangs,
They laugh and twirl, oh how it hangs!

With capes and twirls, they fly around,
Their laughter echoes without a sound.
Like dandelions on a spree,
They scatter joy, oh can't you see?

They juggle dreams and silly schemes,
Spinning tales like wild, sweet creams.
With a wink, they break the mold,
These women fierce, with hearts of gold.

So raise a glass to those who glide,
On winds of humor, full of pride.
With every gust, they dare to play,
Bringing sunshine to every day!

The Sky's Embrace

The sky whispers secrets with a laugh,
Tickling clouds as they swim and quaff.
I traded my shoes for a silly kite,
Now I bounce in the breeze, what a sight!

With cotton candy fluffs above,
The sun plays matchmaker to love.
Stars wear sunglasses, such a show,
As comets dance with the moon, oh no!

Rain showers giggle with delight,
Puddles form before my flight.
Jumping high, I splash and fly,
While puddles send splashes to the sky.

So here's to skies that tickle and tease,
With soft winds and fun that never cease.
In this vast world of silly motifs,
We find joy like lost and found beliefs.

The Harbingers of Hope

A flock of pigeons in a parade,
Wearing tiny hats, oh what a charade!
They coo and clap, with flair and flair,
Sprinkling giggles on the air!

With every flap, they send a cheer,
Bringing sunshine when skies are drear.
These feathered folks with playful ways,
Dance through life in endless plays.

They sing of dreams and ticklish tales,
As laughter flutters and never fails.
With quirks and quirks, they strut so bold,
Carrying wishes, stories untold.

So here's a toast to those who soar,
With funny hats, forevermore.
In the sky's embrace, we find delight,
With harbingers of hope in every flight.

Luminescent Clouds of Peace

In the sky, fluffy clouds dance,
With giggles that seem to prance.
They tickle the world below,
Spreading laughs like a soft glow.

Puffy pillows in a blue sea,
Cracking jokes with great glee.
They whisper in the sun's embrace,
Floating around, a merry chase.

They tumble and turn on a whim,
Caught in a playful, joyous hymn.
With every bounce, they draw a smile,
Raining happiness for a while.

Each puff a promise, soft and light,
Filling hearts with pure delight.
No worries here, just gentle fun,
In the sky, we all are one.

The Serenity of the Aether

In the realms where laughter flies,
Bubbles rise and bounce like pies.
Joy drifts on a cotton breeze,
Tickling sense like playful tease.

Stars check in with a bright hello,
While comets put on a funny show.
In a space where giggles soar,
Serenity dances, wanting more.

Cosmic jokes and chuckles burst,
This universe is filled with thirst.
For joy that spins like a bright top,
In the quiet, let the laughter hop.

A place where woes just float away,
And spirits stumble in a play.
Amid the calm, there's so much cheer,
Join the giggles, the time is here.

A Journey Beyond

Pack your bags with snacks and cheer,
We're off to a land so dear.
Where the silliness rules the day,
And every critter loves to play.

Through valleys where the funny streams,
Flowing wildly, bursting dreams.
Each step's a dancing gig, you see,
Join the fun with glee and glee.

Donuts roll and tacos twirl,
Around the trees, they skip and whirl.
With every laugh, we venture more,
On this journey, endless lore.

So grab a friend, let's hit the road,
With joy and laughter, light the load.
Across horizons wide and bright,
Let's share the chuckles, pure delight.

Weightless Whispers of Love

In a world where whispers jest,
Love floats by, a bubbly fest.
Tickling hearts with every word,
Happiness sung, softly stirred.

A gentle breeze sends notes that soar,
Light as air, they kiss the floor.
Every whisper, sweet and bright,
Brings laughter dancing in the night.

With every giggle, affection glows,
In the quiet, joy bestows.
Light and airy, love takes flight,
Whispered secrets in moonlight.

So let's twirl in this soft embrace,
With laughter lighting up the space.
In playful antics, we shall find,
Love that dances, fun entwined.

Shades of Intended Bliss

In a world where chickens prance,
They dance a jig, oh what a chance!
With each cluck and squawk a hearty cheer,
Plucking worries, never fear.

A duck in boots, how very neat,
Struts around on tiny feet.
With hats that twirl and bags so bright,
They pull a prank, what a sight!

A parrot tells a silly joke,
With every word, the laughter stoked.
They mimic all, from high to low,
While chortling, they steal the show.

In this land of whirligigs,
Where jigs are danced by wiggly pigs,
The skies are filled with carefree glee,
Come join the fun, you'll see, you'll see!

A Mosaic of Seraphim

If angels wore a silly hat,
Would they still sparkle in their chat?
With roller skates and bows so bright,
They'll zip around, what a delight!

One twirls around on cotton clouds,
While others sit, forming proud crowds.
They sip on juice from silver cups,
And giggle loud as laughter erupts.

They play hopscotch on the moon's glow,
Skip past stars in an endless flow.
With feathers mixed in every hue,
Their spirit sings, forever true.

As giggles rise to the sky so blue,
In a dance, they bring joy anew.
Life's a ball in this wacky land,
With seraphs dancing, hand in hand!

The Whispering Winds of Time

Windy whispers flow with glee,
Tickling all, even the tree.
They swirl around in a joyful twirl,
As squirrels laugh, and leaves all whirl.

A breeze sneaks past, gives a nudge,
Making feathers ruffle, not a grudge.
In the park, all critters play,
Chasing clouds that drift away.

The breeze tells tales of silly things,
Of dancing kings and flying rings.
With quirky jokes and funny rhymes,
Time flies in these breezy climes.

So lift your spirits, let them soar,
In winds that knock upon your door.
Join the dance in this playful game,
With laughter sweet, nothing's the same!

The Elysium Between Us

In a garden where giggles bloom,
Bouncing bunnies spread the room.
With floppy ears and pinkish tails,
They hop around, sharing tales.

A cat adorned with shades so cool,
Winks at birds that flit like a fool.
They strut around, making a scene,
Laughing together, oh what a dream!

Together we dance on daisies bright,
With butterflies joining in delight.
Their laughter floats, a joyful tune,
As we sway beneath the sunny moon.

In our playful sanctuary,
Joy and giggles don't get scary.
With every joke and all the fun,
It's a world where we all can run!

The Lullaby of This Life

When morning breaks, I hear a song,
A tune of socks that don't belong.
My cat leaps high, dodging a shoe,
While my coffee spills—it's nothing new.

The toaster pops, a dance in place,
Cheerios fly with such grace.
I chase the dog, who steals my snack,
In this circus life, there's no turning back.

The clock ticks slow, yet time feels fast,
As I reminisce on the silly past.
Each moment's a jig, so twist and shout,
In this grand old life, what's it all about?

So here's a cheer, raise your cup high,
For laughter that lifts, like birds in the sky.
With joy in each stumble, embrace the play,
In this lullaby of life, let's dance away.

A Dream's Delicate Embrace

In dreams, I fly on spaghetti strands,
A noodle ship with wobbly hands.
I greet a fish who wears a hat,
And we debate if cats or dogs are fat.

Clouds made of candy drift and sway,
Each gumdrop gliding in a silly ballet.
I trip on pillows; oh, what a sight,
As unicorns tap dance under moonlight.

A dragon sneezes confetti galore,
While I steal a snack from a slumbering boar.
The tickle of giggles fills the air,
As my dreams swirl in a whimsical flare.

Catch me, O night, in your fluffy embrace,
While I chase rainbow rabbits in a dreamy race.
In every adventure where laughter flows,
I'm just a kid in a world that glows.

Horizons of Infinite Possibility

Beyond the hills where the odd socks roam,
Lie treasures of misfit toys and foam.
I ride a bubble, pop and soar,
Through lands of jellybeans and more.

Here, time is silly; it's never straight,
With rubber chickens dictating fate.
I traverse lands in my fluffy shoes,
Where ice cream rains and you can't lose.

The sun beams giggles, painting the sky,
While vegetables dance and spiders fly.
Each step is an 'oops' and every glance,
A chance to wobble in a silly dance.

So, grab your cap and let's explorate,
With a wink and a grin—no room for hate.
In this land of whimsy, come take a stroll,
Horizons await, full of laughter and soul.

The Breaking of Daylight Wings

As dawn slips in with a goofy grin,
Waking up the sleepy wear and tear kin.
The sun pops out, a big, bright face,
Racing down the sky at a frantic pace.

Birds in pajamas flit and dive,
In a match of chases, oh so alive!
Each chirp's a pun wrapped in delight,
As I sip my tea, what a silly sight!

Morning giggles skip on the dew,
While squirrels gossip like they always do.
Handstands in branches, what a bold show,
These critters put on a jousting faux.

So let's embrace this break of day,
With laughter and joy in a vibrant array.
Together we'll flutter, twist, and sing,
On the wings of mornings, let our hearts swing.

Celestial Dust and Timeless Dreams

In a world where cows can fly,
I once asked why, they looked at the sky.
With twinkling stars stuck in their hooves,
They danced on clouds, oh how they grooved.

A potato in space, what a sight,
It spins and twirls, oh, what a delight!
While wearing a helmet made of cheese,
It shouts to the moon, "Pleased to meet!"

Lollipops rain from marshmallow trees,
As gumdrops grow just as you please.
A tickle of joy in every bite,
The universe giggles, what a night!

So let's don our hats, all shapes and hues,
And waltz through the cosmos with silly shoes.
With celestial dust glimmering wide,
We'll laugh at the stars as they take us for a ride.

Shadows of the Carefree

In a world where shadows play hide and seek,
They giggle and wiggle, it's quite the peek.
A shadow of a cat with a top hat grand,
Offers you ice cream right from his hand.

The sun spills laughter on open fields,
As daisies spin tales that the wild winds yield.
A butterfly sneezed at a ticklish flower,
Causing a chain of giggles to shower.

A knock-knock joke sent through the breeze,
Made all the trees shake with laughter and ease.
With each giddy breeze comes a tickle of cheer,
In shadows of fun, let's all disappear!

So gather your giggles, and whirls of delight,
In the dance of the carefree, life feels just right.
With whimsy as our compass, we'll wander and play,
As shadows twirl happy in their joyful ballet.

Lightness in Through the Veil

In a land where the cats wear turtlenecks tight,
They hold comedy shows every Thursday night.
Pat the dog acts as the clown with flair,
While the fishes in bowls beg to be part of the air.

A veil of giggles, a sprinkle of glee,
Makes even the grumpiest grumpy old tree.
With rustling leaves speaking kooky rhymes,
They chuckle together, defying all crimes.

Down the rabbit hole, we tumble and twirl,
Chasing the sun in a silly whirl.
Gummy bears juggling their fruity delight,
Welcoming all to the oddest of nights.

With laughter as currency, let's roam through the light,
In this realm where the whimsical feels so right.
Through the veil of great joy, let's kick off our shoes,
And dance with the shadows, we've got nothing to lose!

The Elevation of Stillness

Picture a turtle on a skateboard zooming,
Taking a break while the whole world's booming.
A snail in shades, sips lemonade slow,
While pondering life and its curious flow.

A bubble floats by, with giggles inside,
It pops to spread joy, no reason to hide.
The teddy bears waltz with their bow ties and flair,
And sprout from the ground, making everyone stare.

Wind chimes are whispering secrets of fun,
As ladybugs glide under the warm sun.
A slice of horizons, so vivid and bright,
Turns stillness to laughter, it's pure delight.

So let us thrum softly in the quiet delight,
Celebrate stillness, our hearts taking flight.
In the elevation of moments both silly and sweet,
We find our pure joy in life's whimsical beat.

Whispers of the Heart's Plumage

In a land where giggles play,
The birds all wear a feathered toupee.
They dance and twirl on the lawn,
Singing songs from dusk till dawn.

A parrot lost in the market fair,
Traded jokes with a bewildered bear.
They chuckled loud beneath the sun,
Feathers ruffled, oh what fun!

With a wink and a flap, they'd compete,
To tell the tale of the funniest feat.
And with each laugh, they felt so bold,
In a world where silliness never grows old.

So let your heart soar high and free,
In a world filled with whimsy, come see!
For every cackle and grin you impart,
Wraps your spirit in a feathered heart.

Wings of Serenity Unfurled

The ducks in tuxedos waddle by,
While flamingos audition for the sky.
They strut about with such flair,
A feathered fashion show, none can compare.

A turkey tried to tell a joke,
But instead, he just made the crowd choke.
With every flub and silly quirk,
They embraced the laughter, it's how they lurk.

The owls hoot puns from their tree,
Making young critters shout, 'Oh, glee!'
Each flap and giggle spreads delight,
As they showcase their whimsy in flight.

Renew your spirit, let laughter be,
As birds spread joy merrily.
With each tickle from the beak of bliss,
Dive into fun, you won't want to miss!

Echoes of the Celestial Nest

In a nest filled with flapping glee,
The young ones chirp in harmony.
"Who made this fine nest with such flair?"
"Not me, I just sat in a chair!"

With a wiggle and wobble, they take to the sky,
Challenging clouds to a silly pie fly.
Giggles resound like a joyful refrain,
As a comet speeds by, adding to the gain.

A starling jokes about the moon's wig,
Stumbling over a hiccup, what a big dig!
Laughter echoes through the night air,
With each feather drift, worries flare.

So gather round in the soft twilight,
Let your laughter fill the starry night.
In the nest of humor, we find our gold,
Stories waiting to be chirped, retold.

Luminous Quills of Reflection

In a sea of colors, quills do shine,
Each one a story, a punchline divine.
Parakeets wearing shades of glee,
Declare, "We're the trends of the tree!"

With a pluck and a quack, the ducks unite,
For a talent show under the moonlight.
Their jokes take flight on the breeze,
Spreading laughter, as warm as cheese.

The nightingale belts out a silly tune,
Ruffling feathers beneath the moon.
As all gather 'round for a chuckle or two,
A bobtail cat joins in; it's a whole new crew!

Reflect on the joy that life can bring,
When every quirk makes your heart sing.
In this feathered carnival, take a stroll,
Dance with laughter to brighten your soul.

Rainbowed Dreams at Dusk

In twilight's glow, where shadows play,
A parrot's joke comes out to stay.
With colors bright and laughter loud,
It paints the sky, oh what a crowd!

The squirrels grin from tree to tree,
While dancing ants hum their decree.
A rainbow dance on sleepy grass,
Where dreams and giggles freely pass.

A dog takes flight on wings of cheer,
Chasing shadows, drawing near.
The moon begins to wink and tease,
As stars join in with comic ease.

Oh nighttime whimsy, soft and light,
Where every chuckle takes to flight.
In dusk's embrace, all fears dissolve,
With silly dreams, the heart resolve.

Untamed Air and Heartstrings

A breeze comes blowing through the park,
Tickling toes, igniting spark.
A kite gets caught in tree's embrace,
As kids all laugh, the winds will race.

A ladybug makes quite the fuss,
Claiming leaves, oh what a plus!
With every gust, a giggle flies,
While pigeons dance in goofy ties.

The clouds puff up in whimsy's glee,
Wobbling like jelly, wild and free.
And owls hoot laughter from afar,
While fireflies strut like shining stars.

In tangled air, we find the tune,
Of joyous hearts beneath the moon.
For every blunder brings a cheer,
In untamed winds, there's naught to fear.

Timeless Grace in the Wind

Giraffes wear hats as breezes swirl,
Pirouetting in a twirling whirl.
While turtles trot with elegance rare,
Acting like they're in a fair.

Light as a thought, a feathered song,
Balloons afloat where we belong.
The laughing leaves in spinning jest,
Tell tales of whimsy, we are blessed.

Two squirrels race on a pogo stick,
What fun they have, their antics quick!
The air is filled with giggly grace,
In timeless fun, life's merry chase.

With every gust, a silly flip,
As laughter twirls on each next trip.
In windswept joy, we play our part,
With timeless grace and open heart.

Fleeting Moments of Elysium

In the park of dreams where giggles bloom,
Squirrels trade hats inside a room.
With tiny umbrellas, frogs take a leap,
In a puddle of laughter, they dive deep.

A cat with shades lounges in the sun,
Plotting mischief, oh what fun!
While flowers giggle, tickled by bees,
A world of whimsy floats on the breeze.

A hiccup from a duck, a joyful sound,
As butterflies dance all around.
Moments fleeting but filled with grace,
In Elysium's joy, each smile we trace.

So here we gather, a motley crew,
Sharing laughter, pure, and true.
In fleeting moments, life's delight,
We find our joy in silly flight.

Whispers in the Wind

A gusty puff with laughter calls,
It teases twirls and jolly sprawls.
Clouds wave at birds, who giggle mad,
As socks and hats just drift and add.

Autumn leaves join in the play,
With every twist, they sway away.
An acorn rolls, a chipmunk grins,
While squirrels plot their autumn wins.

In silly gusts, the grasses dance,
As butterflies take a wild prance.
A breeze so spry, it lifts my mood,
And hiccups through the neighborhood.

So giggle with the howling air,
As whispers float without a care.
A chuckle here, a snicker there,
With nature's joy beyond compare.

The Tern's Silent Song

A tern that thinks it sings so sweet,
Flops on the sand with foolish feet.
Its vocal range is quite a mess,
Yet every squawk brings forth a guess.

It flaps about in silly style,
With antics that could stretch a mile.
While folks all stop to take a glance,
At the bird that sparkles in its dance.

As waves come crashing, sounds combine,
A cacophony of laugh divine.
The clumsy bird with flappy wings,
Turns drama into summer flings.

So next you see that zany tern,
Just laugh aloud, and take your turn.
For every silence packed with cheer,
Might make a tune you want to hear.

A Cascade of Charmed Breaths

With every breeze a tickle traced,
A magic swirl takes up the space.
It tumbles by with giggles in tow,
As clouds crack jokes and feathers flow.

The trees all laugh, their branches sway,
Creating quips throughout the day.
While daisies dance, their heads agree,
That fun should be the only spree.

Bubbles rise up from ponds that cheer,
As laughter softens every fear.
Each breath cascades, a sight so sweet,
A chorus of joys that can't be beat.

So take a spin on that wild air,
Join in the fun, beyond compare.
A merry breeze, a silly shout,
In the playful world, we roam about.

Elysian Wings on the Breeze

Wings that flutter in raucous flight,
Bumping through clouds in sheer delight.
They dance past trees with silly grins,
And laugh aloud as mischief spins.

Every flap's a giggle shared,
With jests and japes completely aired.
A sideways swoop, a dippy dive,
Brings forth a twist, the birds contrive.

Down near the pond, a splash, a leap,
As frogs croak rhymes, the echoes keep.
And all around, the sprites partake,
While gentle winds wiggle and shake.

So when you see those wings at play,
Join in the laugh, don't shy away.
For in this whirl of air and fun,
Life's zany moments have just begun.

A Mosaic of Wings and Whispers

In my pocket, a bird took a nap,
Said it wanted to fly, but missed the map.
A hat on its head, all funny and neat,
Tried to look dapper, but shuffled its feet.

The pigeons conspired, quite bold and loud,
They planned to take over and draw a crowd.
With breadcrumbs as bribes, they gathered in teams,
Oh, the hijinks that played in their whimsical dreams.

A duck with a banjo strummed tunes in delight,
While chickens taught jazz in the glow of moonlight.
In a world so absurd, with birds on parade,
Every giggle and chuckle was wonderfully made.

So let's dance with the sparrows, and laugh till we cry,
As the world spins in feathers, we all learn to fly.
In the grand scheme of laughter, we take to the sky,
Join the jolly troupe of winged whimsy on high.

The Heart's Feathered Echo

A parrot stood guard, it swore like a sailor,
With tales of the ocean, it was quite the trailer.
It mimicked the sounds of a phone's silly ring,
Leaving its owner without anything.

A robin dreamed big, of dancing on toes,
But tripped on a worm, much to its own woes.
It pirouetted, then stumbled, oh what a show,
Leaving onlookers in fits of laughter aglow.

The hawks had a meeting, plans for world fame,
But forgot their speeches, so they played a game.
Of tag and of leapfrog, they flapped with such glee,
In a feathered fiasco, so joyful and free.

With wings made of giggles and hearts filled with cheer,
These birds of the air brought whimsy near.
In this echo of laughter, we find our way home,
With every light-hearted flapping, we wander and roam.

Winds of Change and Clouded Skies

A kite caught the breeze, on a rather wild quest,
With ribbons and colors, it fancied a jest.
It twirled through the clouds, like a kid on a spree,
But tangled with laughter, and hung from a tree.

The owls had a meeting, at midnight they'd dine,
On pizza and doughnuts, with fizzy grape wine.
They debated and hooted, such wisdom they shared,
But forgot where they sat, and no one really cared.

A flock of young sparrows dared each other, you see,
To race to the fence post and back while still free.
With flapping and flailing, they hustled and flew,
In a dizzying circle, they didn't know what to do.

So when winds begin swirling, and skies turn to gray,
Find joy in the chaos, let laughter hold sway.
For with every mad moment, the world spins a tale,
Of windy adventures and whimsical trails.

Grace Among the Echoed Skylines

A flamingo once strutted with style so divine,
Wore shades and a scarf, said, "I'm feeling fine!"
It danced through the park, with a high-flying flair,
While ducks cracked up, rolling round in midair.

The starlings performed, in a flash-mob surprise,
With moves that would dazzle and light up the skies.
In a flurry of feathers, they twirled and they spun,
Like a party of chaos, oh look what they've won!

The swallows recited poetic bird rhymes,
Of love found in worms and the best loony times.
They lauded the sunshine, the rain, and the breeze,
In endless hilarity, they brought us to our knees.

So as you take flight, to the land of the bold,
Remember the laughter, the stories retold.
With grace among echoes, let giggles take flight,
For in this grand journey, we find pure delight.

A Tapestry of Grace

In a world of fabric fun,
Threads of laughter under the sun.
Tickled by breezes, they sway and dance,
Crafting joy with every glance.

Bobbing like ducks in a grand parade,
Slapstick mishaps, no plans are made.
Screeching colors, wildly bright,
A tapestry woven in goofy delight.

Sunshine sprouts in every stitch,
Whirling and twirling, just a little glitch.
Crafty hands stitch the silly and sly,
Creating smiles as the moments fly.

So here we are, under the sky so blue,
Playful designs, a whimsical view.
With every laugh, a thread we embrace,
In this quirky life, we find our place.

Emblems of the Invisible

A crow in a top hat, oh what a sight,
Conducting a symphony, day turns to night.
Invisible laughter floats in the air,
Imagination's spark hidden everywhere.

Dancing shadows play peek-a-boo,
While giggles twirl like a fun little crew.
Mysteries wrapped in a riddle or two,
The absurd and the wacky always come through.

Invisible hats and whimsical shoes,
Adventures await in hilarious hues.
Jesters and clowns invite us to play,
With each funny emblem, they brighten our day.

So let's celebrate the curiosities found,
In the silly antics that life has around.
With laughter as our invisible guide,
We dance through the whims with sparkling pride.

Soft Murmurs Above the Clouds

Balloons whisper secrets on cottony skies,
Iridescent dreams that take to the highs.
With a giggle here and a chuckle there,
The clouds burst with laughter, a fluffy affair.

Tickling the wind, they get quite a kick,
A weather dance that's clever and quick.
Chasing the raindrops, they twirl and glide,
Bringing joy as they merrily slide.

Puffing up giggles like sweet cotton candy,
Floating along, feeling bright and dandy.
Silly companions in the breeze they bring,
Creating a symphony, soft clouds that sing.

So let's soar high, beyond the ground,
In a sky where mirth and folly abound.
With every soft murmur, let joy be found,
Life's whimsical dance is where we're unbound.

The Lightness Within

A pogo stick heart that jumps with glee,
Cracking up laughter, so wild and free.
With every bounce, a chuckle ignites,
Bringing joy to the silliest heights.

Bubblegum dreams float high in the air,
Made of sprinkles and whimsical flair.
Within every giggle, a lightness grows,
A dance of delight, as happiness flows.

Bright balloons float and pop with cheer,
Each burst sends laughter, oh so dear.
In the silly moments, we find our light,
In the humor and joy that lifts us all night.

So let's laugh loud and jump to the sky,
With unrestrained joy, let's all unify.
For there's a lightness at the heart of our kin,
Where laughter and love make the world spin.

Silent Wings and Hidden Strength

Underneath the couch they lie,
A thousand dreams that laugh and cry.
Jumbled chaos, soft and light,
Dancing shadows in the night.

Plucked from humor, lost in time,
Hiding secrets, mellow rhyme.
Each a tale that wishes to fly,
Yet here they sit—oh my! oh my!

A caper here, a prankster's glee,
Whispers sweet, but rarely free.
Bundled up in a dusty heap,
These hidden strengths just love to sneak.

When you're down, just look around,
The giggles echo, joy unbound.
Lift your spirit, take a peek,
Find the laughter, time to sneak!

The Celestial Ballet

In the night sky, twirls the jest,
Planetary pirouettes are the best.
Stars of chaos spin and glide,
Galaxies chuckle, can't hide their pride.

Dancing comets with tails so bright,
Flipping tricks in the silky night.
A cosmic waltz, laughter's charm,
Who knew stardust could be so warm?

With planets prancing, oh what a scene,
Asteroid twirls in a tutu, so keen!
Even the moon can't help but grin,
As celestial beings start to spin.

Twirling and swirling, oh what fun,
In the universe, we all run.
Every giggle a fleeting spark,
In the grand ballet of light and dark!

Lanterns of the Unseen

Hidden lanterns, bright and cheery,
Guide the way, though they seem eerie.
Bouncing glow, like a gleeful sprite,
Shining beams in the blanket of night.

Behind closed doors, the laughter waits,
In the shadows, it contemplates.
Tickling ankles, making a fuss,
Those sneaky ghosts just want to bust!

Illuminated giggles, they dance in the dark,
Wit and whimsy leaving a mark.
Each bright glimmer a tickle on the soul,
Every flicker hides a humorous goal.

So let them shine, those lanterns rare,
In the unseen corners, let laughter flare.
With a wink and a nod, they beckon us near,
To join in the fun and spread the cheer!

Echoes of Wishes Captured

Wishes bounce on playful streams,
Gathering echoes of wild dreams.
Each little giggle captured in time,
A whirl of whimsy, a chatty mime.

Sailing on air, they hum a tune,
Tickling the pink clouds of the afternoon.
Wishing wells and teetering frogs,
All join in with giggly smogs.

Oh, the echoes that swirl about,
Chasing shadows, spreading doubt.
With every chuckle, wishes take flight,
And bubble around in sheer delight.

So toss your hopes into the breeze,
Join the laughter, let it tease.
For in each echo, find a shade,
Of dreams alive, never to fade!

Serene Hues of Freedom

In a world where pigeons dance,
A ballet of clucks and chance.
With each hop and clatter near,
They make the mundane disappear.

Socks mismatched, they strut so bold,
Grinning wide, never old.
Cafés cheer their daily show,
As crumbs rain down from above, oh no!

Their tales told with a wild flair,
Of lost breadcrumbs, a feathery care.
Who knew they could have such fun?
Dressed for a party, they outshine the sun!

In all their nonsense, joy does bloom,
Gliding gracefully from room to room.
Freedom's laugh echoing clear,
With a little fluff, they spread good cheer!

Songs of Aerial Whispers

High above in skyward chats,
The chirpers hoot, the fliers bat.
They plot comedies in the blue,
Trading secrets, just a few.

"Who ordered these seeds?" one squawks,
"Not me, I swear!" another talks.
Belly laughs from feathered throats,
Sharing jokes that make no notes.

It's a riot in the air so high,
As they flit and flutter, zooming by.
Flapping flags of vibrant hue,
Sprinkling giggles like morning dew.

With every swoop and dive they take,
Life's better with a feathered shake.
Their nonsense lifts the world around,
In feathered antics, joy is found!

Celestial Wings Unfurled

Fluffy clouds become their stage,
As they engage in feathered rage!
They twirl and dive in style so grand,
With silly struts upon the land.

One crow insists he's quite the chef,
With wormy stew, his own twist, no less!
The robins chuckle, "What a sight!"
In this kooky cook-off, it's pure delight!

Up high with antics, they do proclaim,
A life of laughter, their kind of game.
Flapping wings let giggles fly,
As they spread joy through the sky.

No serious acts, just pure delight,
In their rambunctious feathered flight.
As they swirl and dive in playful spree,
Colors burst like a fun jamboree!

The Spirit's Gentle Ascension

On the breeze, they gently tease,
With wobbly flights that aim to please.
Chasing dreams with a wiggle and sway,
In a dance that brightens the grey.

"Look at me!" cries one with flair,
"As I misjudge this windy air!"
With spins and dips, they tumble down,
Rolling in giggles, don't wear a frown!

Daring plummets mixed with grace,
As they flaunt their silly race.
In their playful, carefree gaze,
Lies a peace that sets hearts ablaze.

So let them fly, this nifty crew,
With laughter loud and skies so blue.
A gentle spirit in every beat,
Their flight gives life a whimsical treat!

Dance of the Silken Breeze

In a world where fluff meets grace,
A chicken danced, quite out of place.
Twirling on toes, it took a chance,
Wings flapping wildly in a silly trance.

With a wiggle and squawk, it stole the show,
As ducks watched on with a curious glow.
They quacked, they waddled, a flurry of fun,
In this comical dance, no one would shun.

The grass was the stage, the sky was the roof,
A clumsy ballet, provided the proof.
Every fowl fluffed up, donned a bright crown,
In this frolicsome sheen, no one wore a frown.

When the sun dipped low, and the giggles soared,
Our barnyard friends thanked the breeze they adored.
With feathers so loud and hearts full of cheer,
They whispered a secret—let's dance every year!

The Feathered Promise

Once a very wise old owl,
Promised to teach a fluffy cow.
With wings of wisdom, this cow did plead,
To master the flight, to succeed the need.

Off they went, side by side,
The owl soared high, while the cow just sighed.
"Jump and flap! Let's give it a whirl!"
But the cow just mooed, and began to twirl.

Down by the pond, with a splash and a glee,
The lesson turned wacky as wacky can be.
The cow leapt over rocks—what a sight!
As the owl just laughed at her clumsy flight.

In the end, with feathers and fun,
They realized their joy had just begun.
Flying was fleeting, but friendship was gold,
In tales of the silly, their bond would be told.

Wings Cradled in Shadows

Beneath the moon, a bat took flight,
Chasing whispers replaced by light.
With a giggle and flip, it tried to soar,
But bumped into walls, oh, what a chore!

A parrot laughed, perched high on a tree,
"You need guidance, come dance with me!"
Round and around, they swooped and glided,
Amid the laughter, no one bemoaned or chided.

The bat misunderstood, started to moonwalk,
With its flappy wings, it made the trees rock.
Twists and turns in the cool night air,
The finest of performers, all without a care.

As shadows grew long, the dance wore on,
The sun held its breath near the crack of dawn.
With a flap and a twirl, all was well,
Just two silly friends, free from the shell.

Notes from a Celestial Choir

In the night, a chorus sang,
With geese, and ducks, and even the pang.
A harmony spun from the ruffles and gruffs,
Together they chimed, and oh, what a fluff!

The stars above tapped out a beat,
As owls hooted soft, their tune was sweet.
But the eagles, proud, with looks so grand,
Tripped over notes not carefully planned.

They soared too high, with a hefty yelp,
While the chickens just clucked, alluding to help.
Amidst the giggles, confusion reigned,
An orchestra born, in laughter it trained.

Now each year, at that magical hour,
The feathered ones gather, wielding their power.
To raise up a ruckus, a symphonic spree,
Their notes ringing bright, wild, and free!

Threads of Color in Flight

In pastel skies where pigeons prance,
Each plume a hue, they've got the chance.
They twirl and loop with silly glee,
Painting the air for all to see.

A parrot squawks, a laugh outright,
Tangled up in a comical flight.
With every flap, a giggle grows,
A rainbow scatter where the wind blows.

They wear their gowns of feathered cheer,
Strutting their stuff without a fear.
With every turn, a chance for jest,
Silly birds, the color fest!

In this wild chase, there's joy in play,
Tickled by wind, they drift away.
A world of hues, in chuckles spun,
Oh, how we smile, just like them, run!

The Spirit's Mosaic

A jester bird upon a branch,
In quirky tights, it takes a chance.
Each pluck and preen, a funny sight,
Dancing shadows in the fading light.

Sapphire crowns and ruby tails,
With silly steps, it never fails.
A mixtape tune of chirps and squeaks,
In mismatched styles, the comedy peaks.

The wind plays tricks, a grand delusion,
As birds perform a wobbly fusion.
With each little hop, they seem to say,
'Join in the fun, come dance and play!'

They twirl and twist in feathered fashion,
A giggling chorus born from passion.
In this mosaic made of mirth,
Who knew the sky could be so berth?

Glimmers of a Feathered Past

Once there was a peacock bold,
With tales of feathers, bright and gold.
He strutted 'round with pomp and flair,
While others giggled at his air.

A crow chimed in, "Oh what a sight!
You think you're fancy? Not quite right!"
They swap their jokes and share their jest,
A feathery roast at their behest.

With every tale, the laughter swells,
As stories shift like ocean swells.
A clutch of birds, both sly and spry,
Reviving legends, oh how they fly!

Through shimmered beaks, the echoes ring,
Of bygone days and silly fling.
In the twilight glow, they take a bow,
As past and present dance somehow.

The Dance of Air and Heart

Two sparrows spin, a dizzy dance,
In twinkling steps, they take a chance.
With every beat, they chase the sun,
Such playful moves, oh what a fun!

A wind gust sways them, giggles rise,
They flip and flop, a sweet surprise.
In rhythmic flutters, hearts in sync,
What joy, what laughter, if you think!

They craft a tune with chirps and squeals,
Twisting tales with each spin's wheels.
In circles wide and loops so free,
They share the bliss of harmony.

And in this merry twirl of flight,
They teach us all to find delight.
Through breath and beat, let laughter sail,
In the dance of life, we shall prevail!

Radiant Quills Adrift in Time

Waddling ducks in hats that shine,
They quack in sync at half-past nine.
With mustaches made of pasta threads,
They dance around like silly blokes' heads.

Down by the pond, they spin and twirl,
In tiny boats, they give a whirl.
Chasing ripples with laughter bright,
Who knew quacking could be such a sight?

With each frolic, the sun begins to rise,
While moonbeams giggle, hiding their surprise.
The clouds wear glasses, a jolly crew,
As time takes flight in a wacky view.

So let's embrace this quirky jam,
Where ducks wear hats, and cows say "Glam!"
In this absurdity, joy we'll find,
With every chuckle, the heart unwinds.

Shimmering Ashes of Soaring Thoughts

Fleeting wishes soar on broomsticks,
Singing loudly, throwing their tricks.
With each laugh, they scatter their dreams,
In a flurry of sparkles, or so it seems.

Half-baked ideas in a quirky brew,
Giggling ghosts in a silly hue.
They float about, a whimsical band,
Painting the skies with a free, mad hand.

Banana peels toss through the air,
As squirrels plot – oh, beware, take care!
While thunder claps with a silly cheer,
It's just the clouds trying not to steer.

So let's celebrate with wild, bright glee,
For life's a game that's kooky, you see!
With shimmering ashes and laughter so loud,
We'll twirl and whirl with the fun-loving crowd.

Wings of Unwritten Verses

A chicken struts wearing purple shoes,
Telling tales of the wildest news.
While mice in glasses debate and bicker,
As time ticks away, getting quicker and quicker.

The breakfast table a circus to see,
With pancakes flapping, so carefree.
Each syrupy smile and jellybean joke,
Turns to laughter as the toast begins to croak.

In a world where quips take unexpected flight,
And cats wear bow ties, posing just right.
Their tails a tale of whimsy and cheer,
As the coffee pot giggles, "Hey, grab a beer!"

Together we write the craziest lines,
With winky faces and silly designs.
In unwritten verses, we soar and glide,
In laughter and joy, we'll take each stride.

Souls Adorned in Celestial Fabric

A parrot wearing polka dots flies,
Giving high-fives and cheeky replies.
While rabbits in ties hop to their beat,
Wiggling their ears to the rhythm of feet.

Clouds made of cotton candy fluff,
Smiling down like, "Isn't this stuff tough?"
With sprinkles of laughter raining around,
While gumdrops dance on the colorful ground.

In this land where fun does abound,
The stars twinkle in a cosmic round.
As we twirl 'neath the cosmic embrace,
Creating giggles in this limitless space.

So fear not the zany, the wacky, the wild,
For joy is just laughter's swaddled child.
With souls adorned in hues of delight,
Let's soar together through day and night.

Kindred Echoes Above

In a world where chickens dream,
They plot and scheme in feathery gleam.
Trying to fly but they just can't soar,
Clucking their tales, oh what a lore!

The roosters practice their morning calls,
While geese honk at the mall's tall walls.
They wander about with great delight,
Blooping and flapping, what a sight!

Pigeons strut in their haute couture,
Looking for crumbs, neat and pure.
They strut their stuff with a silly flair,
Dropping their snacks everywhere!

And when the sun begins to set,
All birds gather for a royal bet.
Who'll be the first to steal the show?
In this feathered realm, just watch them go!

Enchanted Wings Bathed in Light

Wizard owls with glasses on,
Counting stars until the dawn.
They trade jokes with the wise old crows,
Chortles echo as laughter flows.

In a parakeet café, oh so bright,
Birds sip nectar, what a sight!
With hats on their heads and ties so neat,
They giggle and squawk, they're hard to beat.

Blue jays dance in a merry band,
Spinning around, isn't it grand?
While cardinals break out their finest tunes,
Jiving along under the moon.

With wings that shimmer, sparkling bright,
They catapult into the night.
And if you listen very closely,
You'll find their joy, so comically!

Ascent Beyond the Fray

A seagull tried to win a race,
But ended up with a silly face.
Flapping upwards, it looked all around,
Then crash-landed on the ground!

Ducks take turns with their splashing flair,
Waddling proud without a care.
In the pond they have their splash contest,
The winner yells, 'I am the best!'

Sparrows chirp in a raucous crew,
Making plans to pursue their zoo.
They want a swing and a seesaw too,
'Cause being small just won't do!

Then down they go for an afternoon nap,
Tangled in branches, what a mishap!
But as they dream of their glorious flight,
They snicker and snore through the night!

Softly Floating Memories

A wren remembers its silly jump,
Flipping around with a mighty thump.
It recalls how it fluffed up with pride,
Only to land on a squirrel's ride!

In a park where laughter blends,
Canaries sing with unexpected bends.
A joke about nuts sends them in a spin,
As laughter erupts from beak to fin.

The joy of a pine cone, chewed with glee,
Brings a chuckle to the busy bee.
They swap tales of the great nut heist,
Then share a giggle, oh what a feast!

As dusk falls, they reminisce and share,
Adventures of quirks in the crisp air.
The light of the moon brings smiles so bright,
To memories woven in soft, silly flight!

Transcendence through Tattered Wings

A pigeon strolls like it's a king,
With ruffled robes, it tries to sing.
Each flap a dance, each strut a jest,
In the park, it calls, "I'm the best!"

A sparrow hops on a fence post,
Telling tales of the coast to coast.
With a chip and a chuckle, it makes its claim,
"I've flown to fame, but none know my name!"

The gulls swoop down for a playful dive,
Counting crumbs, they're so alive.
In a whirl and twirl, they spin and glide,
Launching laughs with each stomach slide.

So here's to the jesters that soar on high,
With tattered wings, they reach the sky.
In the air, humor knows no bounds,
Where every flap is laughter that resounds.

The Art of Floating Gossamer

A moth thinks it's a star on stage,
Dancing close to the flickering page.
It pirouettes on a lazy breeze,
Unaware it's aiming for the cheese!

In a gust, a butterfly flops and flares,
Crashing into petals, unaware of stares.
"Oops! I'm just painting the air in style,"
It giggles and shakes, sporting a smile.

With a twirl like a child on a swing,
It finds the luck in a light-hearted fling.
"Who says I can't get where I want?"
As it bumps the tulips, leaving them gaunt.

So here's to the art of joyous flight,
Where wings are the brush under sunlight.
Every bumbling drift is a scene to behold,
Crafting laughter, bright and bold.

When Spirits Take Flight

A crow wears shades – looking real cool,
Cawing secrets, breaking the rule.
It struts and glares at every cat,
"You think you're sly? Check out my hat!"

In the trees, a parakeet tells a tale,
Of daring escapes and a nightingale.
"I sang so sweet, I stole the show,"
With flair, it boasts, puffing up, aglow.

When the sun begins to set its light,
Birds gather round for a flighty fright.
They take off laughing in a wild chase,
Like a game of tag in this open space.

Under the moon, they giggle and glide,
With spirits soaring, all fear subside.
In the night sky, they find their delight,
Chasing shadows 'til the morning light.

A Canvas of Soft Horizons

A seagull's laugh echoes on the shore,
Dipping and diving, who could ask for more?
It squawks to a crab with a wink and a nod,
"Old pal, let's strut, it's us against the fraud!"

With a splash, it dances through the wet,
Kicking up waves, not one bit upset.
"Freedom is funny when you play it right,"
It fluffs its feathers to take flight.

In this soft scene where colors blend,
Birds paint the sky, laughter won't end.
Each stroke of a wing, a giggle takes form,
Creating horizons where humor is warm.

So let's raise a toast to those who roam,
In a sky so vast, always calling it home.
With wings wide open, they brush away woes,
A canvas of joy in every wind that blows.

The Weightlessness of Being Free

In a world where socks don't match,
And chairs become thrones of the lazy batch.
I float like a cloud, light as a breeze,
With dreams in my pockets, I do as I please.

Bouncing on pillows, a trampoline's friend,
I rally the laughter, no need to pretend.
A dance with the dust bunnies, oh what a sight,
Who knew freedom's weight was so feather-light?

A unicorn jumps, on my head there's a hat,
With jellybeans showering, imagine that!
I trade in my worries for giggles and glee,
In a realm of the silly, I'm wild and free.

So let's toast to the moments where fun reigns supreme,
Where life's just a waltz and laughter's the theme.
No maps for our journey, just joy as we roam,
In this whimsical world, I've truly found home.

Enigma of the Whispering Skies

Above, clouds gossip in the bright, blue sea,
They share the secrets of what it means to be.
One claims to be a sandwich, another a shoe,
In the sky's crazy kitchen, what a stew!

I hear the rain giggle, waiting to fall,
As it tickles the rooftops and dances with all.
Lightning holds court, with thunder on drums,
The clouds throw a party; who knew they had funs?

The sun slides a grin, all golden and proud,
While a chicken belches, lost in the cloud.
A flurry of socks, parade in the air,
Clearly, these skies don't have a care.

So let's toast to the mysteries wrapped in fluffy grace,
The whimsical whispers that play in this space.
With skies of delight, we'll take to the high seas,
Chasing giggles and puzzles blown gently by breeze.

Whispers of Broken Wings

Once there was a bird, with a wing made of toast,
He soared through the air, a buttery ghost.
But on a dippy morning, with jam in the breeze,
He flapped and he floundered, stuck in the trees.

He chirped to his friends, from branches overhead,
Singing sweet songs of a breakfast gone bread.
They laughed till they rolled, what a silly sight,
A toast-laden tale that sparkled with light.

Then came the butterfly, with glittery flair,
She danced through the air like she hadn't a care.
"Wings can be silly!" she spun with delight,
While toast-bird just giggled, feeling just right.

So, laugh with the lost, join the clumsy and free,
In a world where our dreams are as light as can be.
With crumbs on our wings, we'll take every chance,
To flap through our whims in a wobbly dance.

The Soft Caress of Dreaming

In a land made of marshmallows, fluffy and sweet,
I stroll through a path where the giggles repeat.
I jump on each soft cloud, it tickles my chin,
What magic unfolds when the dreamers begin.

My shoes made of sparkles, each step lights a smile,
I slide down the rainbows, oh, come join the while!
With fairies that chuckle, and dragons that play,
We skip on the moonbeams until break of day.

The dreams whisper secrets in swirls of pure cream,
The world is a canvas, draped soft in a beam.
So bring your oddities, your laughter and cheer,
In this land of the dreaming, there's nothing to fear.

So grab a cloud cupcake, and dance with delight,
Let's paint the whole sky with joy, love, and light.
For in the realm of dreams, we can laugh and explore,
Creating our tales, let our spirits soar.

Soft Breeze

The wind whispers jokes as it floats by,
A tickle on cheeks, oh my, oh my!
It carries giggles from tree to tree,
A playful dance, wild and free.

With each gust, the leaves do sway,
As if they're clapping, joining the play.
The clouds above chuckle in delight,
As they change shape, a whimsical sight.

Birds join in with chirps and caws,
They strut and preen without a pause.
In this dance, the world feels light,
What a laugh, oh what a sight!

So come and twirl in this soft breeze,
Let joy and laughter float with ease.
For in each gust, we find our glee,
In nature's jest, we are truly free.

Soft Thoughts

Pillow dreams on a lazy day,
Cuddle up, let worries stray.
Thoughts as fluffy as clouds above,
Tickling minds with gentle love.

A giggle sneaks through sleepy heads,
Spreading warmth like cozy beds.
What if cats did stand-up shows?
Or if fish wore fancy clothes?

Silly riddles dance like mist,
In this world, you can't resist.
Let imagination take its flight,
Soft thoughts bloom, bringing delight.

With soft laughter echoing wide,
Feelings gentle, hearts open wide.
In this space, let worries cease,
Soft thoughts invite the sweetest peace.

The Embrace of Avian Dreams

What if birds sang opera loud?
Mice in tuxedos, oh so proud!
Chirping tenors with stunning flair,
In the sky, musical air!

Imagine nests made of candy floss,
Hatching eggs with chocolate toss.
Feathers tickling the dreams at night,
As birds serenade the moonlight bright.

A parade of ducks in a fancy fair,
Waddling to tunes without a care.
With goofy beaks and silly shoes,
They dance away, spreading good news!

In dreams, our fowl friends come alive,
With laughter, joy, and fun to thrive.
So, let's take a trip in this bliss,
To realms where whimsy cannot miss.

Plumage of Tranquility

In the garden where the laughter grows,
A plump pigeon strikes a pose.
With a fluffed-up chest and goofy grin,
He claims the throne—the king of skin!

Swaying flowers laugh at his charm,
As bees buzz around, causing alarm.
But our king stands regal, unfazed,
Wearing his crown of pollen, amazed!

The sun tickles petals in pure delight,
Spreading warmth, a friendly light.
Each bloom dances with vibrant cheer,
Joyful whispers fill the air here.

In this realm of colorful bliss,
Even the ants join in the kiss.
Tranquility wrapped in hues so bright,
A silly world painted in sheer delight.

Silken Notes on Winter's Breath

When winter whispers, all is still,
But snowflakes dance, what a thrill!
Each flake a note, a melody clear,
Singing softly for all to hear.

Squirrels wear coats, oh what a sight,
As they scurry about, pure delight.
They're plotting snowball fights galore,
Whiskers twitch, they're ready to roar!

Frosty laughter fills the fresh, crisp air,
As penguins slide without a care.
A ballet on ice, a whimsical show,
Winter's breath makes spirits glow!

So gather 'round, let joy accrue,
In the chill, find warmth anew.
For even when the cold winds blow,
Laughter echoes, and spirits grow!

www.ingramcontent.com/pod-product-compliance
Lightning Source LLC
Chambersburg PA
CBHW060110230426
43661CB00003B/145